Other books by Ben-Tzion Spitz

Fiction

- Joshua: Conqueror
- Destiny's Call series:
Book One - Genesis
Book Two – Exodus
Book Three - Leviticus
Book Four – Numbers
Book Five – Deuteronomy

Non-Fiction

- Mikraot Ketanot: Torah Shorts on the Weekly Reading
- Commandments in Color (Hebrew)
- The Oracle and The Rabbi: A Nexus of Art, Bible and Jewish Philosophy
- Jewish Adventure in Modern China

#dafyomi #tweets

BABYLONIAN TALMUD TRACTATE BAVA BATRA

@bentzis
Ben-Tzion Spitz

Valiant Publishing

#dafyomi #tweets
BABYLONIAN TALMUD
TRACTATE BAVA BATRA
@bentzis

Valiant Publishing, 333 West Merrick Road, Suite C
Valley Stream, NY 11580, USA

Author's blog: ben-tzion.com
For schools or bulk orders, contact the author directly at:
bentzispitz@gmail.com
First Edition
1 3 5 7 9 10 8 6 4 2
ISBN 978-1-937623-30-2

To my fellow Daf Yomi companions worldwide.

#definitions

#tweets: Messages sent via online news & social media site "Twitter" @twitter.com, restricted to 140 characters per message.

#dafyomi: lit. "daily page" - daily study by worldwide Jewry of folio of Babylonian Talmud. 2711 folios. Completed in cycle of 7.5 years.

#BabylonianTalmud: Teachings of 1000s of Rabbis from BCE to 5th century, with law, ethics & history. Basis for all codes of Jewish law.

#BavaBatra: 1 of the 63 tractates that comprise the Babylonian Talmud. Deals mostly with property rights & responsibilities.

#purpose

#dafyomi is an incredible worldwide phenomenon, educating and uniting Jews off all streams and backgrounds.

#dafyomi can be a time-consuming, laborious yet intellectually, spiritually and religiously invigorating commitment.

#dafyomi can seem intimidating to people with a weak Jewish education.

#dafyomi is now accessible for people with NO background in translation & w/ excellent explanations & commentaries, in print & online.

#execution

#dafyomi #tweets are for people who want a brief, tiny, initial exposure to the tip of the #BabylonianTalmud iceberg.

#dafyomi #tweets is akin to explaining Einstein's Mass-energy equivalence by merely writing E=mc2. There is significantly more behind it.

#dafyomi #tweets just gives a highlight / folio. It's written in tight shorthand, trying to squeeze a lot of info in < 140 characters.

#dafyomi #tweets can also be a good and fast review for people who've already learned the Daf before.

#technical

#dafyomi #tweets gives the number of each folio before each tweet.

#dafyomi #tweets should arouse your curiosity. Check out the actual Daf online in translation to see what it's really talking about.

#dafyomi #tweets was composed with the help of sefaria.org and dafyomi.co.il. Both resources are highly recommended.

#BavaBatra

2: Ability of a neighbor to have unobstructed view into ones house from outside is considered a damage (Hezek Reiah).

3: Don't demolish a synagogue before you've built its replacement.

4: "The bird of the skies will carry the voice." Don't say anything you wouldn't want repeated to anyone else.

ה

5: Resh Lakish: We don't believe people who say they paid their debt earlier than they had to, without proof.

6: Facing houses: each owner needs to build at least half a length of wall on roof to prevent the other from looking in.

7: Lived in city 12 months, status of resident to pay for city projects. Bought house, considered resident immediately.

8: All punishments come to the world due to ignoramuses. (Kaiser that levied taxes on city, ignoramuses left, pardoned).

ט

9: Whoever gives charity to a poor person receives 6 blessings. Whoever consoles a poor person receives 11 blessings.

10: Debate: TurnusRufus: Giving to poor is against God's wish. R' Akiva: Giving to poor exactly what God wants us to do.

11: Munbaz gave his wealth to charity: "Went up, can't touch, bears fruit, saves souls, benefits me, gets next world."

12: R' Avdimi: After era of Prophets, prophecy given to the wise. R' Yochanan: prophecy given to fools and children.

13: Half-slave, half-free must be freed entirely (so can marry). "World was only created for the sake of reproduction."

14: Authors of Tehilim (Psalms): King David, Adam, MalkiTzedek, Abraham, Moshe, Heiman, Yedutun, Asaf & Korach's 3 sons.

15: R' Yehuda: Joshua wrote last 8 lines of Torah (about Moshe's death). R' Shimon: Moshe wrote it himself in tears.

16: God to Iyov (Job): I didn't err in placement of hair follicles. I didn't err in punishing you. Iyov vs Oyev (enemy).

17: Eden snake killed 4 (they didn't sin): Benjamin, Amram (Moshe's dad), Yishai (David's dad) & Cilav son of David.

יח

#dafyomi #tweets #BavaBatra

18: Must keep 3 Tefah
(handsbreadth) away
from neighbor's wall:
grains, plow, urine.

18

19: R' Nahman: Ditch to soak laundry must be at least 3 Tefah from neighbor, ditch to rub laundry at least 4 Amot away.

20: Can open bakery or dyer's shop under wine storage; smoke improves wine. Can't have animal pen; stench spoils wine.

21: Yehoshua b Gamla stopped Torah being forgotten in Israel. Instituted national school system. Also, 25 kids/teacher.

22: Only acceptable jealousy is that of scholarly accomplishment - increases wisdom. "Kinat sofrim tarbe chochmah."

23: Any indirect damage that someone may cause is still their responsibility and prohibited to allow to happen.

23

24: "A pot owned by partners is neither hot nor cold." If more than one person has responsibility, job doesn't get done.

25: 4 winds always blow, but world can't exist w/o north wind. South wind would destroy world if not for angel Ben Netz.

26: Roots of neighbor's tree are in your field: can cut the roots up to depth of 3 Tefah, so don't block path of plow.

כז

27: Ulla: Square of same length as diameter of circle is 1/4 bigger. Sages: Ulla was not precise (but reasonably close).

28: Hazaka: owner if act as such 3 yrs over: pit, cave, dovecote, bathhouse, olive press, fields, slaves & production.

29: Rava: Human nature: need 3 yrs to establish Hazaka, as one pardons use of their property for 1 or 2 yrs, but not 3.

30: Rava: Normal for person to be busy at market for 30 days & not go home or notice squatter in house during that time.

31: R' Yehuda: Don't establish Kohen with just 1 witness. R' Elazar: If no one argues, can establish Kohen w/ 1 witness.

32: Law like Rabah on land dispute, leave claimant there; like R' Yosef on money dispute, leave money where it is.

33: People aren't so brazen as to harvest a field that isn't theirs or eat food that isn't theirs.

34: If required to take an oath (only 1 witness), but for some reason can't give an oath (not believed), has to pay.

35: R' Ashi: Serial robber
is still called a robber.
Can't atone: stolen object
won't be returned;
doesn't know to who.

36: Ate Orla (prohibited early produce), produce of 7th yr or Kilayim (prohibited mix) doesn't prove owns via Hazaka.

לז

37: R' Zvid: 1st claims trees, 2nd claims land, that's what get. R' Papa: 1st gets trees w/ 1/2 land, 2nd gets 1/2 land.

38: Reason 3yrs for Hazaka: 1yr until people talk about it, 1yr to get word overseas, 1yr for owner to return & protest.

39: If person doesn't have an independent need to keep your secret, will eventually forget that it's secret & reveal it.

40: Should state in front of 2 witnesses: protests; declarations (of duress); admissions (of obligation); acquisitions.

מא

41: Owner: "What are you doing in my field?" Squatter: "I've been here 3 yrs. No one said anything." Not a Hazaka claim.

42: Craftsmen, partners, sharecroppers & overseers can't prove own by Hazaka on property they work on, share or oversee.

43: Torah scroll was stolen from a city: can't use the judges of that city to judge the case as they may be biased.

44: Sold land w/o taking responsibility if taken by creditor, buyer can't make claims. Seller can't give any testimony.

45: If deposited an item in front of witnesses, must be returned in front of witnesses.

46: Took back article from craftsman & discovers not his, can use it until claimed. Took from some gathering, can't use.

47: R' Yochanan: A thief & his son are both disqualified from claiming anything per rules of Hazaka. Grandson can.

48: Divorce bill (Get) forced by non-Jew is valid, but Rabbis prohibited so women shouldn't be dependent on non-Jew.

49: Woman can say to her husband: "Don't take care of me financially, but then you don't get any of my earnings."

50: No Hazaka by damages, can always protest: R' Mari: smoke entering property; R' Zvid: stench reaching neighbor.

51: Sold field to wife: she acquires, he can eat the produce. Gifted field to wife: she acquires, he can't eat produce.

52: Has deposit from child, buy w/ it Segula (produces & principal intact) - R' Hisda: a Torah. Rabah: a date tree.

גג

53: 2 free fields: If takes hold of: field A, acquires it; A to acquire both, just gets A; A to acquire B, gets 0.

54: Shmuel: "dina d'malhuta dina" = Law of the land is the law. King says can only buy land w/ contract, must follow.

55: When determining Peah (leaving corner of field to poor), divided by river, stream, public or private road or path.

56: Hazuva: trees Joshua planted to mark land borders. Roots go straight down & don't nurture from other's property.

57: Hazaka of land not accomplished by: leaving one's animal there, setting up oven or millstone, or raising chickens.

58: A wise man only places his shoes under his bed. An ignoramus has a whole storehouse under his bed.

59: If drainpipe drips water into neighbor's yard, owner can't block the pipe & neighbor can protest if does.

60: Rabbis can't make a decree that most of the people will not be able to handle.

61: Sold Zihara (inheritance), includes fields, gardens & vineyards but not houses or slaves; sold "his property", all.

62: In sale of field, borders of the field need to be extremely well defined, otherwise can end up with unusual borders.

63: Sumchus: If said give to so-and-so "part of pit", gets 1/4; "of barrel", 1/8; "of pot", 1/12; "of pitcher", 1/16.

64: Sold house, doesn't include pit/cistern, however, if seller wants to use them, needs rights to path. Sages disagree.

65: Pipe was hollowed out & then attached: like a utensil & disqualifies Mikva if it's waters were filled via the pipe.

66: R' Eliezer: A beehive is like land: doesn't get ritually impure, if remove honey on Shabat, liable. Sages disagree.

67: Sold "Hatzer" (courtyard), includes: houses, pits & caves, not movable objects; unless said "Hatzer & all in it".

68: Sold field, doesn't include unneeded rocks or reeds and unattached grain, unless said "field & everything inside".

69: Rocks that are needed for a field: Sages of Bavel: rocks that hold down sheaves. Ula: rocks arranged like wall.

70: R' Chisda: Borrower believed if said returned loan, if he swears. (He could have said that it was lost blamelessly).

71: R' Akiva: Sold field, doesn't include pit, winery or dovecote, whether empty or full, but must buy path to access.

72: If consecrated to Temple 3 trees spaced out over area of 75,000 amot2, also includes all land & trees between them.

עג

73: If sold ship, includes mast, sail, anchors & oars, but not slaves, bags for merchandise or merchandise.

74: 2 crevices w/ smoke where Korach & his group were swallowed. They chant: "Moshe & his Torah are true. We are liars."

75: Rav: Pulling a ship any amount acquires it. Shmuel: One must pull the ship its own length to acquire it.

76: R' Papa: When sell documents, must write in document to transfer ownership: "acquire it & all the liens it creates."

77: Sold wagon, didn't include mules; mules, didn't include wagon; yoke, didn't include oxen; oxen, didn't include yoke.

78: Calculation of the World: calculating the cost of doing a Mitzva vs the reward; the gain of sin vs what will lose.

79: R' Yehuda: whoever separates from Torah is consumed by fire. R' Dimi: whoever separates from Torah falls to Gehinom.

80: Bought tree in order to cut it down, must cut a handbreadth above ground in order to allow the tree to grow again.

81: Bought 2 trees, doesn't acquire land w/ it. Bought 3, does & owns whatever grows from stump & roots & can replant.

82: R' Hiya b Aba: Bought 3 trees, acquires land. Includes under & between trees & area around for harvester & basket.

83: Sold head of large animal, legs not included; legs, head not included; lung, liver not included; liver, no lung.

84: Sun is white, but red morning & evening. Rays pass through roses of Gan Eden in AM & through entry of Gehinom in PM.

85: Buyer's utensil acquires whatever is placed in it wherever he's allowed to place the utensil (not in public domain).

86: Buyer brought seller's workers w/ fruit into his house, if didn't set price AND measure fruit, either can retract.

87: Can't pay discounted wage before start of work; discount looks like charging interest. Once started working, fine.

88: Sages: Borrowing without permission is like stealing. Must return to owner (& not just return to where took from).

89: Place where normally sell even measure, don't sell heaping measure & vice-versa; even if says will adjust the price.

90: It's prohibited to hoard life-essential products, such as wine, oil and flour, to sell later at a higher price.

צא

91: Elimelech, Mahlon & Kilyon (from Ruth) were the leaders & benefactors of generation. Punished for leaving Israel.

92: Rav: Seller sold an ox & it was found to be a gorer, the sale is considered a mistaken sale & is void (Mekach Taut).

צג

93: Liable: grinder didn't soak wheat 1st; baker makes crumbly bread; butcher invalid slaughter. Must compensate buyer.

94: Buyer must accept Rova of legumes per Seah of wheat; Rova straw/Seah barley; Rova dirt/Seah lentils. ~3% impurities.

95: If the Onaah (over- or undercharging) is less than 1/6, sale valid. If more, sale void. If exactly, Onaah returned.

96: Rav: Barrel of wine spoiled: within 3 days, sale invalid. Shmuel: Sale valid, cause is buyer's bad Mazel (fortune).

97: R' Zutra b Tuvia: We don't make Kiddush except with wine that is fit to be used as a libation upon the altar.

98: Lowliest: man who lives in in-laws home; worse, guest who invites other guests; worse, speaks before other finished.

99: R' Levi: Tradition from our ancestors: the Ark & the Cherubs didn't occupy any space at all in the Holy of Holies.

100: No limit to road for a king; breaches fences to make path for himself. No limit to road for funeral; honor of dead.

101: Burial cave: interior size > 4 amot x 6 amot. Kuch (place for coffin): 4 amot long, 7 tefach high, 6 tefach wide.

102: Vineyard w/ < 4 cubits between vines. R' Shimon: Not a vineyard; people don't plant to uproot. Rabbis: Is vineyard.

103: Discussions as to how & if rocks & ditches are included in sale of field: location, size, density, distribution.

104: Discussions as to discrepancies in sale of field, price, size, when field needs to be returned & how much returned.

105: Rental agreement: 12 dinars/year, 1 dinar/month & became leap year (13 months), renter pays 1/2 of added month.

106: Sold stated area within borders, but area turned out to be less. If < 1/6, sale ok. If > 1/6, deducts from price.

107: 3 appraisers, 3 values, use avg. R' Eliezer b R' Tzadok: avg of 2 lowest values. Others: (high - low)/3 + low.

108: Relatives inherit from & bequeath to each other. Some inherit but don't bequeath. Some bequeath but don't inherit.

109: Micha's idolatry: Priest was Yonatan b Gershom b Menashe. Moshe's grandson, but attributed to Menashe, an idolater.

110: Yonatan b Gershom b Menashe later renamed Shevuel b Gershom b Moshe. He repented & returned to God (Shevu-El).

111: Son has precedence over daughter to inherit from their father & from their mother. A husband inherits from wife.

112: R' Yishmael needs 2 verses to prove his points: 1. Husband inherits from wife; 2. Son inherits from mother.

113: R' Avahu: A husband inherits what is Muchzak (owned) by wife, not what is Ra'uy (destined) for wife.

114: Man about to die gave gift, until when retracts? Rabah: as long as parties seated. R' Yosef: as long as discussing.

115: Had precedence in line of inheritance & died, their descendants inherit before anyone else. Father precedes sons.

116: Verse: "Those that have no exchange & fear not God." Debate: means left no son after him or means left no student.

117: R' Shimon: Land of Israel allocated based on who left Egypt as well as who entered Israel. Fulfills both verses.

118: Advice: Downplay success. Avoids Evil Eye of others, which can cause harm. Doesn't apply to Joseph's descendants.

119: R' Chisda: In general, woman marries < 20, can bear children until 60. > 20, can bear until 40. > 40, won't bear.

120: R' Ami: In matters of Torah, we give priority to the greatest sage; at a banquet, priority goes to oldest person.

121: 7 men's lives span all history: Adam, Metushelah, Shem, Jacob, Amram, Achiyah Ha'Shiloni & Elijah, who still lives.

122: Tribal lots originally assigned by "divine lottery." High Priest Elazar used Urim V'tumim to match tribes to lots.

123: Jacob to Rachel: I'm your father's match in trickery. Can a Tzadik deceive? Yes, permissible to deceive a deceiver.

124: Rebbi: Firstborn gets double portion of gains after father's death, but not of those due to orphan's efforts.

125: R' Papa: Firstborn gets extra share only of what father held, not of what is owed, whether paid with money or land.

126: If father says: "My son, the eldest, will not get 2x portion; my son will not inherit with brothers," meaningless.

127: Son known as 1st, dad says different son 1st, believe dad. Son known as not 1st, dad says is, don't believe dad.

128: Valid witness & saw testimony, but became deaf, blind, insane, related, invalid. Returned to original status, ok.

129: Divided estate, gave to some more & others less, if did so as a gift, binding. If did so as inheritance, invalid.

130: Don't learn Halacha (Law) from what was taught or from a ruling unless Rabbi said: This is the Halacha in practice.

131: "Benin Dichrin": sons you'll have from me will inherit your Ketuba above their share w/ brothers from other wives.

132: Man told son died, wrote his property to others, son not dead, gift void. If knew son alive, wouldn't have given.

133: Gifted property to others, didn't leave any for sons, valid, but Sages upset. R' Shimon: If sons were improper, ok.

134: Any gift where the giver has expectations or demands as to how the recipient should use the gift is not a gift.

135: Person died & a Daitiki (gift document of a Shechiv Mera, a person about to die) found tied to his thigh, ignore.

136: Man wrote property to son for after death, man can't sell it 'cuz going to son. Son can't sell because still dad's.

137: R' Yehuda: Man wrote property to friend but doesn't want it, even if screams, he acquires it. R' Yochanan: Doesn't.

138: R' Aba: R' Yochanan: protested from beginning, gift not valid; R' Yehuda: was 1st quiet then protested, gift valid.

139: Father gave property to son, gives generously, son receives whatever is attached. Sold to stranger, only gets land.

140: Rava: on limited inheritance, first $ separated to feed daughters until adulthood & whatever is left to feed sons.

141: R' Chisda: 1st child a girl, good sign: helps raise future children; no Evil Eye (jealousy, male 1stborn gets x2).

142: Convert died without heirs, people grabbed his property, heard that had son or pregnant wife, must return property.

143: R' Ami: man sent silk clothes home, sons get male clothes, daughter female clothes. If daughter-in-laws, also get.

144: R' Safra, great scholar, wouldn't take time from learning to labor for other's benefit. Proof work for own profit.

145: Shushvinus laws: can sue for; repay when giver marries; no interest; Shmita doesn't cancel; 1stborn doesn't get x2.

146: Shmuel: changing ones regular diet (even if it's to more & richer food), is the beginning of stomach illness.

147: Shemini Atzeret look at Altar smoke: if wind from S, much rain; N, little rain; W, everyone happy; E, everyone sad.

148: Shchiv Mera wrote all property to others: if was initial intent, they acquire post-death; if recovers can retract.

149: "Any amount" left by Shchiv Mera: enough land to support himself; enough movable property to support himself.

150: Giving away all property: Shchiv Mera, can retract; to slave, goes free; to wife, oversees; for evasion, invalid.

151: "Property" includes: animals, birds, tefilin. Unresolved if also Torah scroll: can't sell except to learn or marry.

152: Shechiv Mera gift says acquisition was made, has 2nd advantage that also like gift of healthy man, can't retract.

153: Gift document says "in life & death": Rav: Shechiv Mera, gets after death. Shmuel: gets while alive. Law like Rav.

154: To take money from giver, need proof. R' Huna: need witnesses that giver was healthy. R' Hisda: validate document.

155: How old need to be to sell property inherited from dad? (Both quoting R' Nachman) Rava: 18. R' Huna b Chinana 20.

156: Gave property verbally, sick or healthy: land acquired via $, contract or Chazaka; all else, by lifting, Meshicha.

157: Rav & Shmuel: a loan without a document can't be collected from the heirs or from person who bought from borrower.

158: House fell & killed couple. Heirs of husband & heirs of wife say other 1 died 1st. Debate how to split inheritance.

159: Ruben sold his dad's property in lifetime & died, dad died, Ruben's son takes from buyers. He's granpa's heir.

160: "Matter established w/ 2 or 3 witnesses." 2 witnesses for regular Get (sign inside), 3 for tied Get (sign outside).

161: Sages' symbols for signing: Rav:fish; R' Chanina:branch; R' Chisda:samech; R' Hoshaya:ayin; Rabah b R' Huna:mast.

162: If 4 or 5 witnesses sign a document, but 1 of them was a relative or invalid witness, still valid due to others.

163: 2 blank lines invalidate document: way witnesses write, not scribes, 'cuz swindler can't write as small as scribe.

164: Said will be Nazerite
Hena = 1 30 day period;
Digon= 2 (60 days),
Trigon/3/90 days;
Tetrigon/4/120;
Pentigon/5/150.

165: R' Yehuda/Rav:
Most people transgress
some theft, a minority sin
in illicit relations & all sin
in some gossip.

166: Birds for sacrifice selling @ 1 gold dinar. R' Shimon: 1 sacrifice/woman enough. Price fell to 1/4 silver dinar.

167: Birurin & court actions only written w/ consent of both parties & both pay scribe. R' Shimon: both get copies.

168: Court tears documents: R' Yehuda: tear place of witnesses, date & Toref (names, amount). Abaye: length & width.

169: Claims lost document of sale, write another w/o Acharayut (compensation guarantee). No to 2 documents for 1 field.

170: R' Huna/Rav: Law not like R' Yehuda or R' Yosi. Court rips old loan document, writes new one with original date.

171: R' Yosi: Keep old loan doc & give receipt if paid part of loan. Makes pay rest fast & collect basis original date.

172: Men w/ same name in same city, use grandpa's name to distinguish. If still same, add other sign to differentiate.

173: Lender only collects of guarantor if borrower has no property, unless stated otherwise. Can collector from broker.

174: Guarantor obligated whether borrower has property or not, except for a Ketuva (marriage contract) never obligated.

175: To become wise, study monetary laws, greatest field in Torah, like a gushing spring. Best to learn from Ben Nanas.

176: Guarantor at time of loan doesn't need Kinyan, but if after, does. In court doesn't need 'cuz likes being trusted.

End Tractate Bava Batra. We shall return to you.

#AboutTheAuthor

#Ben-Tzion Spitz, prolific writer of biblical & rabbinic themes.

#Former Chief Rabbi of Uruguay

#blog at ben-tzion.com

#twitter @bentzis

#publisher: valiantpublishing.com

www.ingramcontent.com/pod-product-compliance
Lightning Source LLC
Chambersburg PA
CBHW020038040426
42331CB00030B/11